max science primary

Workbook 1

DISCOVERING THROUGH ENQUIRY

PAT DOWER

SERIES EDITOR: **BOB KIBBLE**

macmillan education

INTERNATIONAL CURRICULUM

Macmillan Education
4 Crinan Street
London N1 9XW
A division of Springer Nature Limited

Companies and representatives throughout the world

Workbook ISBN 978-1-380-02152-6

First published 2019

Original design by EMC Design Ltd and Macmillan Education
Page make-up by Ink Design
Illustrated by Magriet Brink pp 12, 61, 75; Xandor Nelmapius pp 7, 8, 11, 17, 18, 25, 26, 44, 48, 59, 68, 69, 70, 72, 73, 77; Stephen Wallace pp 5, 10, 30, 35, 47, 54, 58, 60, 83, 85; Anna Hancock c/o Beehive Illustration pp 55, 56, 60; Daniel Limon c/o Beehive Illustration pp 19, 78; Baz Rowell c/o Beehive Illustration pp 20, 82, 86; Ricard Zaplana Ruiz c/o Beehive Illustration pp 77, 83
Cover design by Sparks Publishing Services Ltd and Macmillan Education
Cover illustration by Star Publishing Pte Ltd and Jorge Santillan c/o Beehive Illustration Agency
Picture research by Susannah Jayes

The author and publishers would like to thank the following for permission to reproduce their photographs:
Getty Images/Ingo Armdt p2(grasshopper), Getty Images/Dorling Kindersley p19(plastic spoon), Getty Images/ScottHughesPhotography p2(cat), Getty Images/joecicak p38(robot), Getty Images/Anup Shah/ Minden Pictures p2(ape), Getty Images/Nature Picture Library p2(spider), Getty Images/Mark Newman p39(Picture A), Getty Images/People Images p24(dustmen), Getty Images/Taja Planinc p35(Venus flytrap), Getty Images/tcsaba p54, Getty Images/iStockphoto/Thinkstock/Silfox p2(bird), Getty Images/Stephen Trainoff Ph.D p2(fish), Getty Images/Richard Wahlstrom p39(Picture B); **Jupiter Images** p20(plastic bottles); ©**Royalty-Free**/Corbis p36(Picture B); **Shutterstock**/HiSunnySky p82(tc), Shutterstock/Icrms p35(plant), Shutterstock/Peter Vanco p36(Picture A).

Printed and bound in the Brazil

2024
26

Contents

Introducing *Max Science primary* Workbook

The ***Max Science primary* Workbooks** accompany the **Student Book** for class and home use. All the numbered activities and extension activities found in the Student Book are expanded with clear answer spaces and support. Instructions carefully show if activities are to be done independently, in pairs or in groups.

Practising my science language

Supported activities focus on improving scientific literacy to make the learning of science through the medium of English more accessible.

Extending understanding

Extension questions encourage learners to go a bit further to improve the depth of understanding.

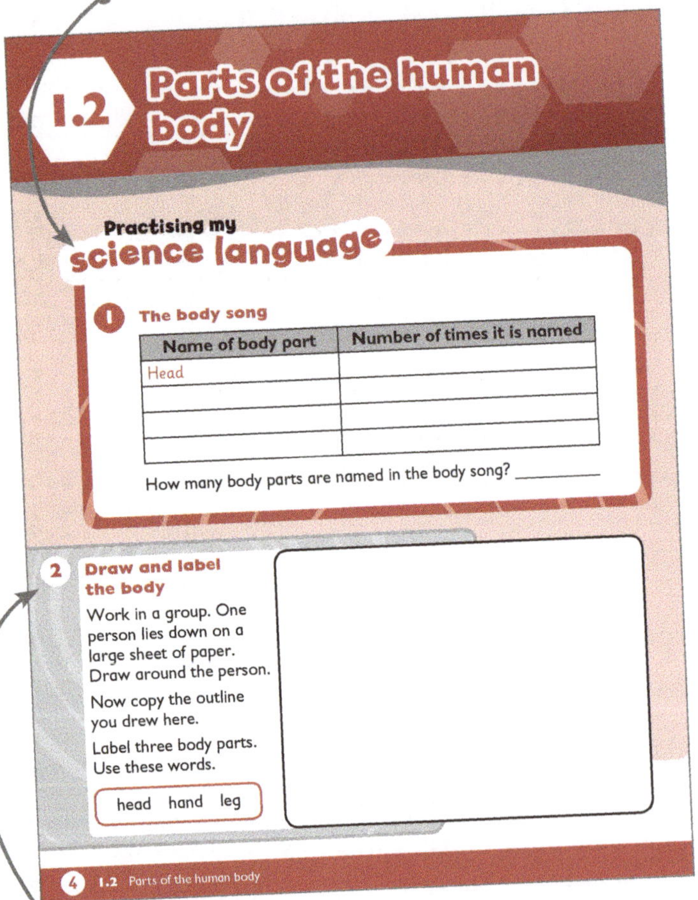

1.2 Parts of the human body

Practising my science language

1 The body song

Name of body part	Number of times it is named
Head	

How many body parts are named in the body song? ________

2 Draw and label the body

Work in a group. One person lies down on a large sheet of paper. Draw around the person.

Now copy the outline you drew here.

Label three body parts. Use these words.

head hand leg

4 1.2 Parts of the human body

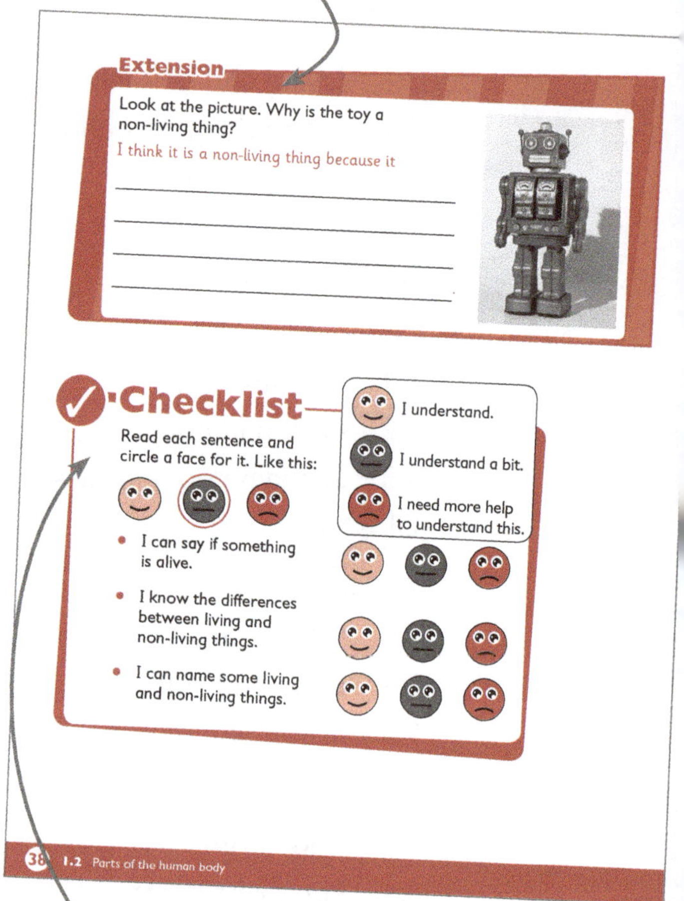

Extension

Look at the picture. Why is the toy a non-living thing?

I think it is a non-living thing because it

Checklist

Read each sentence and circle a face for it. Like this:

I understand.

I understand a bit.

I need more help to understand this.

- I can say if something is alive.
- I know the differences between living and non-living things.
- I can name some living and non-living things.

38 1.2 Parts of the human body

Exploring science further

Numbered activities from the Student Book are expanded with example answers for guidance. Learners can record their scientific progress, insights and results.

Assessing progress

End of topic checklists provide opportunities for recording what learners have learnt so far.

1.1 The human body

Extension

Find out more things about your partner.
Tick the things that are true. ✔

Can you both move?	☐	Do you both grow?	☐
Can you both run?	☐	Are you the same height?	☐
Can you both touch your toes?	☐	Is your hair the same length?	☐

Write two more things that are the same for you and your partner.

We can both ____

____.

Write two more things that are different between you and your partner.

____

____

1 My features

Circle the words for the correct colours for your eyes and hair.

Example: **blue**

My eyes are: **blue** **brown** **green** **none of these**

My hair is: **black** **brown** **blonde** **red**

My shoe size is: ____________.

Make a class chart of your answers with your teacher.

2 Comparing children in my class

Look at the class chart for eyes, hair and shoe size.

How many children have **brown eyes**? ____________

How many children have **brown hair**? ____________

The most common shoe size is ____________________.

Extension

Get into groups. Look at the animal pictures.

How are the animals the same as humans? How are the animals different from humans?

Tick the features that you can see in these animals. ✔

Feature	Ape 	Cat 	Fish 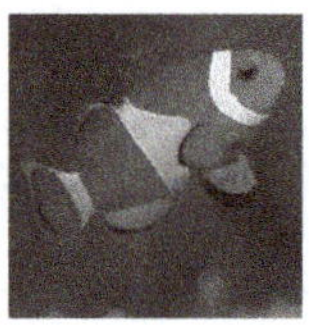	Bird 	Grasshopper 	Spider 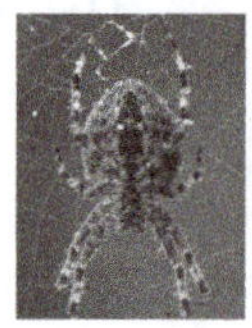
Head						
Eyes						
Ears						
Arms						
Fingers						
Legs						
Toes						
Hair						

Which two animals are most similar to humans? ____________ ____________

Which two animals are least similar to humans? ____________ ____________

3 Sorting human features

Which circle should these features go in?

Write the number in the circle. One has been done for you.

1	A head	**2**	Wings
3	Eyes	**4**	A tail
5	Brown hair	**6**	Blue eyes

All humans have these.

1

No humans have these.

Some humans have these.

1.2 Parts of the human body

Practising my science language

1 The body song

Name of body part	Number of times it is named
Head	

How many body parts are named in the body song? ___________

2 Draw and label the body

Work in a group. One person lies down on a large sheet of paper. Draw around the person.

Now copy the outline you drew here.

Label three body parts. Use these words.

head hand leg

Practising my

science language

Write the labels

Look at this picture.

Write the name of each body part in the box.

Choose from these words:

head toe knee shoulder hand leg ~~foot~~

Now add these labels to your body drawing.

Take it in turns.

Look at the other groups' drawings.

Do you want to change any of your labels?

Extension

Can you label your picture on page 4 with these parts too?

neck hip waist
finger eyelash mouth

Checklist

Read each sentence and circle a face for it. Like this:

- I understand.
- I understand a bit.
- I need more help to understand this.

- I can say how humans are the same.
- I can say how humans can be different.
- I can name parts of the human body.

1.3 Sensing

1

Hearing

Your teacher will make some sounds.

Draw circles around the sounds that you hear. One has been done for you.

stirring a drink in a cup

pouring water

banging a drum

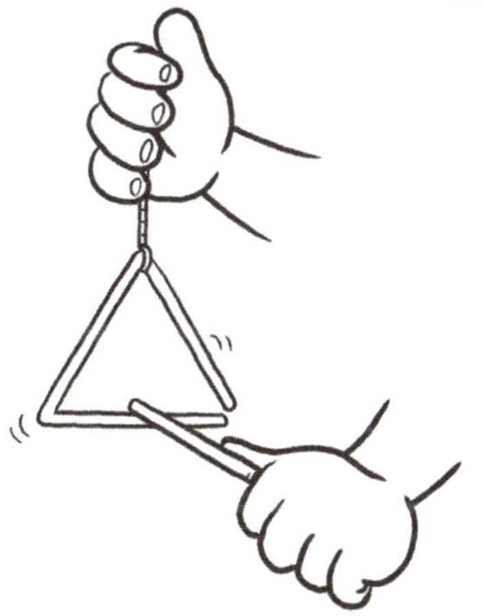

hitting a triangle

shaking a maraca

scrunching paper

2 The “ I spy…” game

Work with a partner. Take it in turns to choose an object.

For a door, say:

“I spy, with my little eye, something beginning with… d.”

The other person tries to guess what you chose.

If you have time, try colour I spy!

Now you do not guess by the first letter of the object, but rather by its colour.

Say:

“I spy, with my little eye, something the colour… **green**.”

The other person tries to guess what you chose. For example:
A **green** plant.

Swap and try it with a different colour.

3 Do you know the smell?

Work with a partner. You are going to smell some objects.

- Wear a blindfold.
- Let your partner move the object past your nose.

Can you guess what the object is by smelling it?

Swap over to try a different object.

	Object 1	Object 2
What do you think the object was?		
What was the object?		
Were you right? ✔ ✘		

What gives your favourite smell? Draw a picture.

My favourite smell is of ______________________________.

4 Guess the food

You are going to taste some foods.

- Work with a partner.
- Wear a blindfold. Your partner will give you a piece of food to taste.

Can you guess what the food is?

Swap over to try a different food.

	Food 1	Food 2
What do you think the food was?		
What was the food?		
Were you right? ✔ ✘		

Think: Did any other sense help you decide what the food could be?

Write your ideas here:

I can decide what the food is by ______________________________

____.

5 What is in the box?

Feel the object in the box. What do you think is inside?

Match the objects in the pictures to the right description.

teddy bear

coin

stick

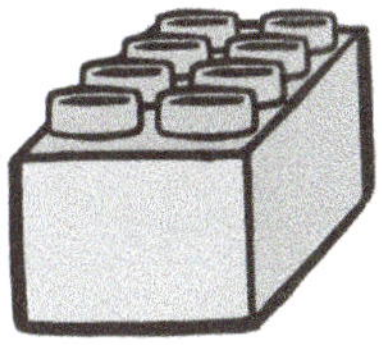

building block

I feel something round and flat.

I think it is a ______________________________.

I feel something long and rough.

I think it is a ______________________________.

I feel something hard and knobbly.

I think it is a ______________________________.

I feel something round and soft.

I think it is a ______________________________.

How many did you get right? ____________

Practising my

science language

6 Name the senses

Write down one of the senses being used in each picture.

Choose from the word box.

The first one has been done for you.

see	hear	feel	taste	smell

When I beat a drum, I can hear it.

When I hold a balloon, I can ________________ it.

When I switch on a fan, I can ________________ it.

When I shine a light, I can ________________ it.

When I ring a bell, I can ________________ it.

Checklist

Read each sentence and circle a face for it. Like this:

I understand.

I understand a bit.

I need more help to understand this.

- I can say what the five senses do.
- I can say what my senses tell me about my surroundings.
- I can say how humans and animals use senses.

Glossary

Write the meaning of these words in your own language.

animal

arms

body

different

ears

eyes

feet (foot)

fingers

grow

hair

hands

head

hear

hearing

human

knees

Glossary

legs

shoulders

mammal

sight

mouth

similar

move

smell

nose

taste

same

toes

see

touch (feel)

senses

2.1 Exploring materials with my senses

1 Talking about materials

Choose two objects that you have been talking about.

Are the objects made from the same material?

Circle your answer. **Yes No**

- Write the name of each object in the table.
- Write what each object is made of.
- Write what the material looks and feels like.

You can choose words from the box or use your own.

shiny metal dull hard smooth rough soft clear cold fabric wood plastic warm

One has been done for you.

Object	What is the object made of?	Description of the material
coin	metal	The material feels hard. The material looks shiny.
		The material feels __________. The material looks __________.
		The material feels __________. The material looks __________.

Extension

Which objects are made from more than one material?

_______________ _______________ _______________

Choose one of these objects. Draw the object in the space.

2 Finding materials

Keira is looking for different materials in her bag, pockets and clothes.

Look for materials in your bag, pockets and clothes.

Draw a circle like this ◯ around the materials you have found.

metal	plastic	stone
wool	paper	
wood	fabric	glass

Did you find any other materials? Circle your answer. **Yes** **No**

If you answered "Yes", write down the name of the material.

____

Practising my

science language

3 Using my sense of touch

Ayesha is feeling the object inside the bag. She is using her sense of touch.

She is trying to guess what the object is made from.

How can she tell the difference between materials?

Plastic will feel ______________________.

Wood will feel ______________________.

Metal will feel ______________________.

The object in Ayesha's bag is a pencil. Which words can Ayesha use to describe the material the pencil is made from? Underline the words she can use. One has been done for you.

soft **<u>hard</u>** **smooth** **rough** **cold** **warm**

Can you think of other words that she can use? Write them here:

____

____

____

____

2.2 What are materials like?

1 **Properties of metal**

These objects are made from **metal**. Tick the words ✔ that describe what metal is like.

soft	☐	breakable	☐	rough	☐
hard	☐	smooth	☐	bendy	☐
strong	☐				

2 **Properties of wood**

These objects are made from **wood**. Tick the words ✔ that describe what wood is like.

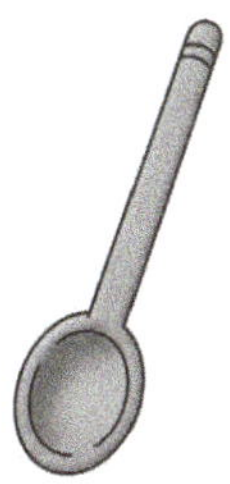
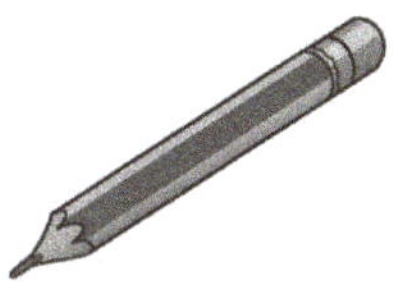

soft	☐	breakable	☐	rough	☐
hard	☐	smooth	☐	bendy	☐
strong	☐				

Extension

What other words describe metal? ______________________________

What other words describe wood? ______________________________

Practising my

science language

3 Guessing materials

Name two materials used to make bottles.
What words describe the materials?

First material: ______________________

Words that describe this material:

____

____

Second material: ____________________

Words that describe this material:

____

____

4 Musical bottles

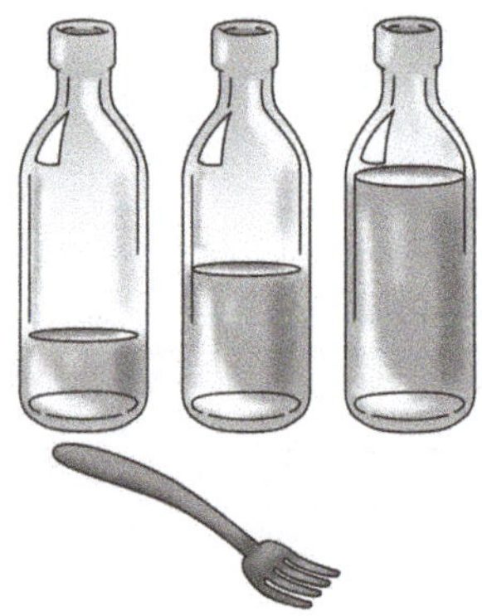

Akim wants to play a tune by softly tapping the bottles with a metal fork. Akim can choose plastic or glass bottles.

Predict which is better: plastic or glass.

My prediction:

I think ______________________ is better.

Test your prediction. Fill a few plastic and glass bottles with different amounts of water. Gently tap the bottles with a metal fork.

Cross out one of the words: My prediction was **right** / **wrong**.

5 **Solving problems**

Choose one of these problems and tick the box ✔ next to it.

1. Keeping firewood out of the rain ☐
2. Making a cat bed ☐
3. Keeping picnic food cool on a hot day ☐
4. Mopping up water on the floor ☐

What material can you use to solve the problem?

I can use ______________________________.

Why did you choose the material?

I chose this material because ______________________________

____

______________________________.

Draw a picture to show how you solved the problem. Label your picture.

6 Comparing materials

Draw and name an object made from these materials.

Stone	Polystyrene
Name of object: ____________	Name of object: ____________
Rubber	**Paper**
Name of object: ____________	Name of object: ____________

How many different objects did you find made from each material?

Stone	☐	Another example: ____________
Polystyrene	☐	Another example: ____________
Rubber	☐	Another example: ____________
Paper	☐	Another example: ____________

✓ Checklist

Read each sentence and circle a face for it. Like this:

- I understand.
- I understand a bit.
- I need more help to understand this.

- I can say what a material is.
- I can name at least five different materials.
- I can use words to describe different materials.
- I can give examples of what the materials are used for.

2.3 Understanding materials

Practising my science language

1 Spotting different materials

Look at this picture.

Circle the **different** materials you can see in the picture.

How many did you find?

____

Describe three of the materials in the table below.

Use the words in the box to help you. One has been done for you.

soft hard strong waterproof bendy
heavy light see-through (transparent)

Material	Words to describe the material
Stone	hard, waterproof, rough

2 Finding materials with specific properties

You ran around to find different kinds of material. What did you find?

A soft material: ______________________________

A hard material: ______________________________

A shiny material: ______________________________

A bendy material: ______________________________

3 Materials for a house

Write which property each of these things needs. Use the words to help you:

soft	bendy	unbreakable	clear
shiny	hard	waterproof	fluffy

Practising my

science language

4 What can materials do?

Your teacher will show you some objects made from materials that do special jobs. Work with a partner to share ideas.

How do the material's properties help each object to do its job?

Put your ideas in this table. One has been done for you.

Example	Name of material	Drawing of object	Properties needed for this job
A pen	Plastic	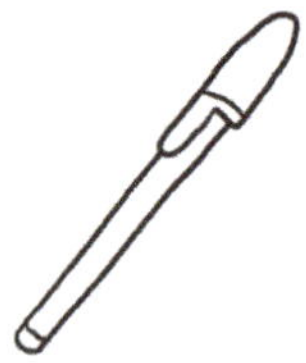	Hard Smooth Light

Extension

You will drop clay balls onto the floor. Make two clay balls.

- Hold one ball up high. Drop it.
- Wrap the other ball in foam. Hold it up high and drop it.

Look at the two balls. Do they look the same? Circle your answer.

The balls look **the same** / **not the same**.

Draw the two balls after they have been dropped.

What job does the foam do?

The foam ____.

2.4 Sorting materials

1 **Sorting into groups**

Look again at the picture on page 29 of the Student Book.
Which materials have the same properties?

Sort the objects into two groups. Draw them here and write their names next to them.

Group 1	Group 2

What properties did you use to sort the materials?

I used ______________________________.

2 Making a sorting poster

Materials I chose for my sorting poster: ______________________

____

____

What properties did you use to sort them? ______________________

____

____

Name **two** other properties that you could have used to sort them:

______________________ and ______________________

Practising my science language

3 Properties game

Make your own properties card game:

- Make a set of cards.
- Write the name of a material on one side of each card.
- On the other side, write the material's properties and uses.

Rules of the game:

1. Turn all the cards over so you can only see the descriptions.
2. Take it in turns.
3. Pick a card and read the description. Can you guess what the material is?
4. Turn the card over. Do not let the others see it! If you guessed right, leave the card name-side up.
5. If you guessed wrong, turn it name-side down and continue the game.

Extension

Look at this list of materials:

metal fabric wood plastic rubber

These materials are used in bicycles and furniture. Some materials are used only for bicycles. Some materials are used only for furniture. Some materials can be used for both.

Write the materials in the sorting circles below.

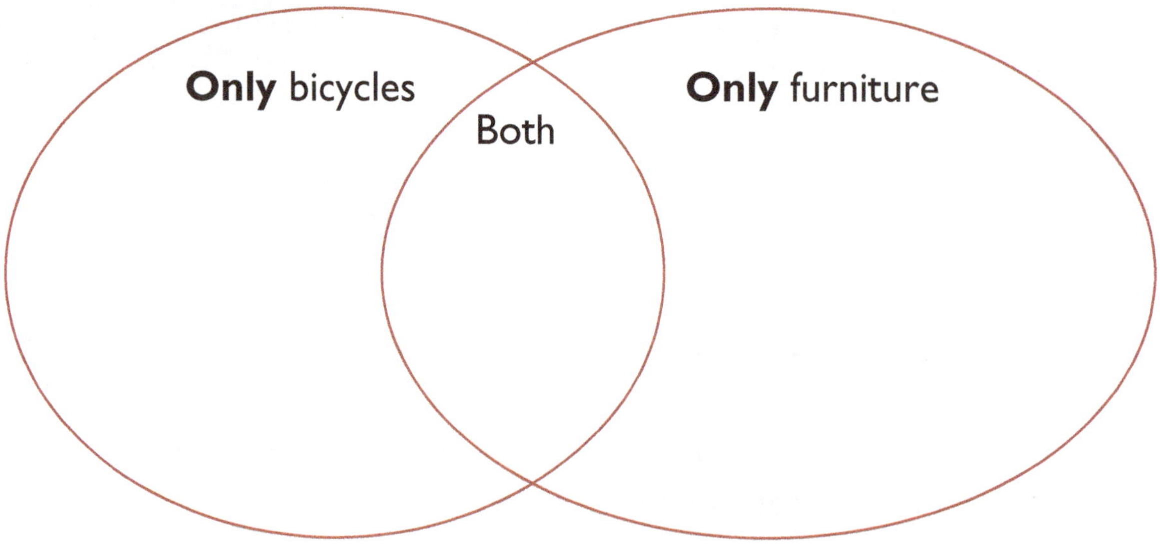

Checklist

Read each sentence and circle a face for it. Like this:

- I understand.
- I understand a bit.
- I need more help to understand this.

- I can explain how materials are used for different jobs.
- I can suggest good materials to use for different jobs.
- I can sort materials in different ways.
- I can use the properties of materials to help me sort them.

Glossary

Write the meaning of these words in your own language.

bendy

different

fabric

foam

glass

group

hard

job

material

metal

nylon

object

paper

plastic

Glossary

polystyrene

properties

rubber

soft

sort

stone

strong

waterproof

wood

3.1 Living and non-living

1 Plants can move and grow

1. Watch the video.

   The Venus flytrap is a special kind of plant.

   - What can the leaves of the plant do?

   ____

   ____

   - Why does the plant do this?

   ____

   ____

   - A Venus flytrap is a small plant. What might happen if it grew as tall as a tree?

   ____

   ____

2. Watch the video of the plant growing. The film is speeded up.

   Describe what you see.

   ____

   ____

Imagine you are a small plant growing into a big one.

Curl up so you are like a small plant and then slowly grow into a big one.

Are you growing in the same way as a plant? Circle your answer.

Yes I am / No I am not

Do you have the same parts as a plant? Circle your answer. **Yes No**

Practising my science language

2 Is this plant real?

Look at the plant in the picture.

How can you tell if a plant is real? Choose a word to fill in the gap.

I can ___ ___ ___ ___ ___ it.

touch	smell	see	taste	hear

Is a real plant a living thing? Circle your answer. **Yes No**

Tick the things that are true for artificial plants. ✔

They look real.	☐	They can have flowers.	☐
They grow.	☐	They need water.	☐
They may feel soft.	☐		

Is an artificial plant a living thing? Circle your answer. **Yes No**

Extension

Look at the pictures.

Which one is the real baby? Circle your answer.

Picture A **Picture B**

Picture A

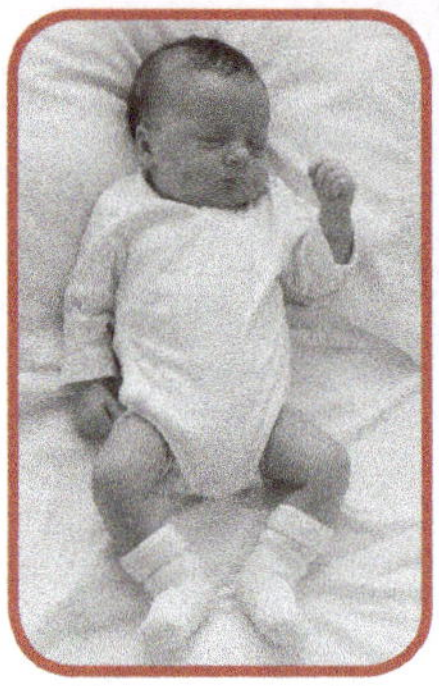

Picture B

Write down why you think this one is the real baby.

I think this one is the real baby because ______________________________

____

____

3 Finding living and non-living things

You walked around the school grounds.

In the space below, draw and name a living thing and a non-living thing you collected on your walk.

Living thing	Non-living thing
Name:	**Name:**

4 **Sorting my collection**

Copy these descriptions into the correct box. One has been done for you.

Can grow	**Can move on their own**	**Do not grow**
Cannot move on their own	**Can have babies**	**Cannot have babies**

Living things	Can move on their own
Non-living things	

Can any of the descriptions go in both boxes?

Circle your answer. **Yes** **No**

Extension

Look at the picture. Why is the toy a non-living thing?

I think it is a non-living thing because it

____

____

____

____

Checklist

I understand.

I understand a bit.

I need more help to understand this.

Read each sentence and circle a face for it. Like this:

- I can say if something is alive.
- I know the differences between living and non-living things.
- I can name some living and non-living things.

3.2 Living things around me

Staying alive

What do living things need to live? Circle the right words beside Picture A.

Picture A

Look at Picture B. Complete the sentence.

Picture B

Things cannot live here because there is no ______________________.

2 Outside learning walk

How many different plants did you see on your walk?

I saw ______________________ different plants.

How many different animals did you see on your walk?

I saw ______________________ different animals.

Practising my science language

3 What is it like where you live?

Complete the sentences.

Here are some words to help you.

sunny	hot	cold	dry	cool	shady	wet	city	town	village

I live in a ______________. Here it is mostly ______________.

Draw a picture of your home.

4 Looking in other places

Watch the video.

- How many different plants can you see? ____________________
- How many different animals can you see? ____________________

What is it like where they live? You can use these words to help you.

light	dark	hot	cold	dry
cool	shady	safe	wet	

It is ____

____

____.

How is it different from the places you saw on your learning walk? Fill in the gaps and circle the correct words.

We went to __________ on our walk. The place in the video is a __________. It is **hotter** / **colder** than where we walked. The place in the video gets **a lot of rain** / **little rain** so it is a **wet** / **dry** place. The plants are **bigger** / **smaller** than what we saw on our walk. There are **many** / **few** animals. The animals are **the same as** / **different from** the ones we saw on our walk.

Practising my

science language

Extension

What is your favourite wild animal?

My favourite wild animal is ____________________.

Describe your favourite animal.

- My animal looks ____________________.
- My animal eats ____________________.
- My animal lives in ____________________.

Draw a picture of your favourite wild animal.

My partner's favourite wild animal is ____________________.

Checklist

Read each sentence and circle a face for it. Like this:

I understand.

I understand a bit.

I need more help to understand this.

- I can say where some plants live.
- I can say where some animals live.

3.3 Eating to live

1 Grouping foods

Your teacher wrote down the names of your favourite foods.

Now write some of those names in these boxes.

Draw lines to show which food goes where.

2 **Food posters**

Make a poster for one of the food groups.

- Write the name of the food group at the top of the sheet.
- Draw or cut out pictures of foods in this food group. Stick them onto the poster.

Write the names of three foods on your poster.

_______________ _______________ _______________

3 **Sugar in drinks**

Can you see the sugar stirred into the water?
Circle your answer. **Yes** **No**

Draw a picture of the drink your teacher shows you.

Guess how many spoons of sugar are in the drink. ☐

Which word is correct? Cross out one of the words:

Too much sugar is **bad** / **good** for your teeth.

What is better? Water or juice? Fill in the gap. ___________ is better.

The healthiest drink of all is fresh _______________.

Extension

Look at the diagram in Activity 1. Think about the foods you eat.

Choose words from the box to complete the sentences.

starchy foods	fruit and vegetables	
meat, eggs or dairy	fatty foods	sugary treats

The foods I eat most are ______________________________

____.

To be healthier I can eat more ___________________________

____

and less ____

____.

What types of food should you eat only a little of?

____

Checklist

I understand.

I understand a bit.

I need more help to understand this.

Read each sentence and circle a face for it. Like this:

- I can say where different foods come from.
- I can name healthy things to eat.
- I can say what is healthy to drink.

3.4 Baby animals

1 **Spotting the mistake**

Look at these pictures. One baby is not with the right parent. Put a cross by this picture.

2 Matching animals and their young

Look at these farm animals. Draw lines to match the mothers with their young animals. One has been done for you.

horse

goat

sheep

hen

cow

kid

calf

chick

lamb

foal

Practising my science language

3 Pets and farm animals

Choose a pet or a farm animal.

Write its name here: ______________________

Think about what the animal was like as a baby.

Circle one from each of these pairs of words:

The baby was **bigger** / **smaller** than its mother.

The baby was **weaker** / **stronger** than its mother.

Can you think of other differences?

The baby was ______________________________________

but the mother was __________________________________.

4 Young humans

How old are you? __________

How old will you be when you become an adult? __________

How many years are there before you will be an adult? __________

5 Human families quiz

Tell your partner about your family.

Ask about their family.

Write your answers in the table below.

	In your family	In your partner's family
Who is the oldest?		
Who is the youngest?		
How many are female?		
How many are male?		
Are there any babies on the way?		
How many generations are alive in your family?		

Practising my

science language

6 Starting questions

Write down one of the questions you asked at the start of this unit.

The question I had was ______________________________.

The answer is ______________________________.

Something else I have learnt is ______________________________

______________________________.

Checklist

Read each sentence and circle a face for it. Like this:

I understand.

I understand a bit.

I need more help to understand this.

- I can compare young animals with their parents.
- I know that families have groups called generations.

Glossary

Write the meaning of these words in your own language.

alive

___

___

animals

___

___

artificial

___

___

cold

___

___

damp

___

___

dead

___

___

drink

___

___

dry

___

___

eat

___

___

family

___

___

farm

___

___

food

___

___

food groups

___

___

generation

___

___

Glossary

healthy

____

____

human

____

____

living

____

____

non-living

____

____

pet

____

____

plants

____

____

real

____

____

water

____

____

young

____

____

4.1 Moving

Practising my science language

1 How does it move?

Complete the sentences about what the car is doing.

You can use words from the box. You can also use your own words.

move	fast	slow	spin	race	turn	skid	forwards	backwards

I see the car ______________________________.

I see the car going ______________________________.

I see the wheels of the car ______________________________.

2 PE drum game

Play the drum game with your class. Now make up your own actions to do when you hear different drum beats.

What are your actions?

- One drum beat: ______________________________
- Two drum beats: ______________________________
- Three drum beats: ______________________________

Practising my

science language

3 Things move in many ways

Choose words from the box to describe the movement of each of the things in the list.

fast	slow	turn	fly	jump	slide
crawl	spin	up	down	glide	

- snail ______________ ______________ ______________
- car ______________ ______________ ______________
- aeroplane ______________ ______________ ______________
- frog ______________ ______________ ______________

What movement is this?

Watch the video clip of a hamster on a wheel.

What kind of movement is it?

____

What other things move like the hamster wheel? Make a list in your group.

____

____

5 Sports

What kinds of movement can you see in these pictures?

Choose from these words:

turning swinging jumping punching hitting
rising falling stretching running

Label each picture. One has been done for you.

jumping, stretching

Checklist

Read each sentence and circle a face for it. Like this:

🙂	I understand.
😐	I understand a bit.
🙁	I need more help to understand this.

- I can spot different types of movement.
- I can name at least three different types of movement.

4.2 Push and pull

Practising my science language

1 Which force?

Which force is needed to move the trolley forwards?

push pull

A __________ is needed to move the trolley forwards.

Which force is needed to move the trolley backwards?

push pull

A ________ is needed to move the trolley backwards.

2 Turning

Look at these pictures or the objects your teacher shows you.

Label each object with the right word from the word box.

key	jar	smartphone	tap	keyboard	box

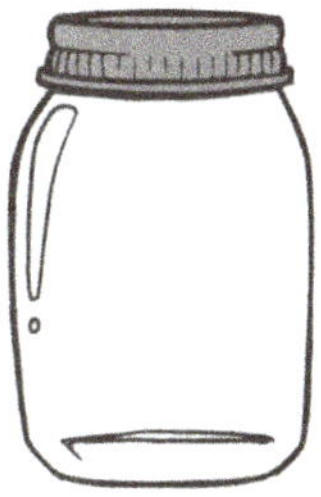

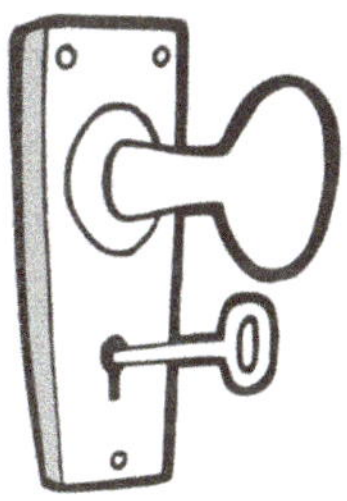

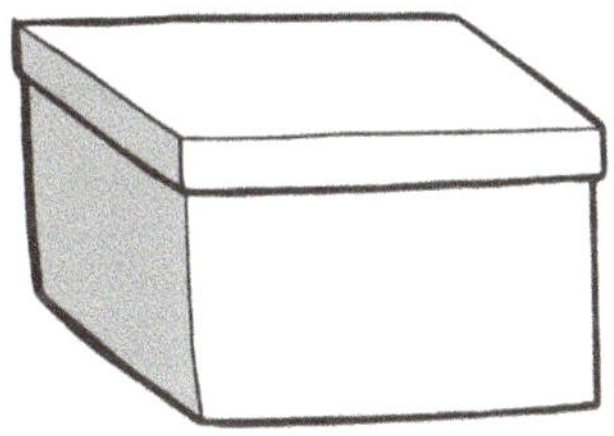

Put a tick (✔) next to the ones that you need a turning force for.

Does everyone in your group have the same answers? Circle your answer. **Yes** **No**

3 Forces at work

Your teacher gave you some objects to look at.

Draw one object. Label the drawing with the forces that made it work.

Choose from these words:

push pull turn twist

4 Faster and slower

Look at the pairs in the pictures.

Which one is going **faster**? Circle your answer.

Which one is going **slower**? Circle your answer.

Does the plane move **faster** or **slower** than the truck?

The plane moves ______________________________ than the truck.

5 Can you make it move?

Try each of these actions. Cross out the part of the sentence that is wrong.

- When I push against a tree, the tree **does** / **does not** move.
- When I pull on a rope tied to the tree, the tree **does** / **does not** move.

Look at the tug of war.

Both boys are pulling. No one is moving.

Why do you think this happens?

____

____

Extension

Circle the correct answers.

Which force is the woman using to put the boxes in the van?

pushing **pulling** **turning**

What force could the woman use if she had no trolley?

pushing **pulling** **turning**

Extension

Do you think moving the boxes is easier with a trolley?
Circle your answer.

Yes **No**

Why?

Because ____

____.

Checklist

I understand.

I understand a bit.

I need more help to understand this.

Read each sentence and circle a face for it. Like this:

- I can talk about different kinds of force.
- I can say what forces do.
- I know that pushes and pulls are kinds of force.

4.3 Speeding up and slowing down

1 The bicycle ride

Use words from the box to label where the movement of the bicycle changes.

speeding up	slowing down	changing direction

2 What makes things move outside?

Circle one word.

The **wind** / **rain** / **sun** makes things move outside.

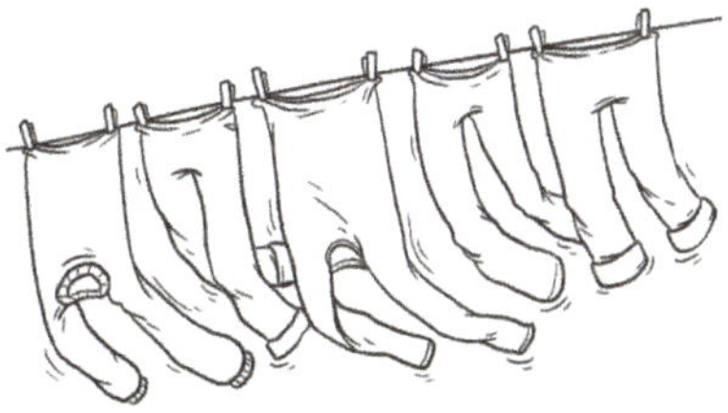

Do things outside always move? Circle your answer.

Yes **No**

Practising my science language

Extension

Gently push a big book across a table. What do you feel?

It feels ______________________________.

Now push the book across a carpet in the same way. How does it feel different?

It feels ______________________________.

3 Rolling marbles

What movement do you see?

____

____

How did you get the marble to stop inside the circle?

I got the marble to stop by ______________________________

______________________________.

What kinds of force were at work?

____

____

4 Changing speed

How did you use the ramp to make the marble roll towards the chalk circle?

Draw a picture to show what you did.

Describe the movement of the marble.

The marble moves ______________________________

______________________________.

When is the marble fastest?

When it is ______________________________

______________________________.

When is the marble slowest?

When it is ______________________________

______________________________.

Checklist

I understand.

I understand a bit.

I need more help to understand this.

Read each sentence and circle a face for it. Like this:

- I can see changes in movement.
- I can compare speeding up and slowing down.
- I can talk about what makes movement change.

Glossary

Write the meaning of these words in your own language.

cause

fast

faster

fastest

force

friction

jump

move, moving

movement

pull

push

slow

slower

slowest

stop

swing

turn

5.1 Where does sound come from?

Practising my science language

1 Making sounds

How are sounds being made in the pictures? Write your answer under each one.

What sounds can you make with your body in other ways?

Write three ideas.

1. ______

2. ______

3. ______

Practising my

science language

Now sing a song. The tune is the same as "Old Macdonald had a farm".

To sing a song you make a sound, move your mouth around.
Listen and you hear some sound, move your ears around.
Sing it softly, sing it loud, sing it when you stand up proud.
To sing a song you make a sound, sounds are all around.

Draw some of the actions that you did for the song about sound. You can draw pictures like this:

Practising my

science language

2 Finding sounds

Look at the pictures. How can you make a sound with each object?

Choose one of these words or a word of your own. Write one word under each picture.

One has been done for you.

bang	hit	shake	rub	pull	push

bang

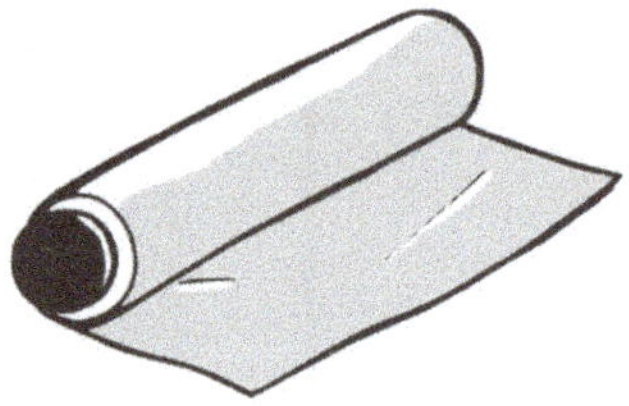

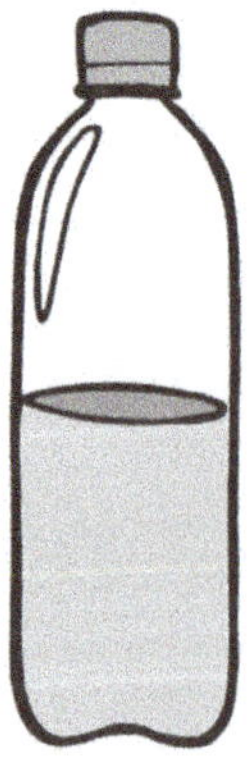

3 Animal sounds

How many different animal sounds did you hear? ____________

Write the names of two animals you heard.

____________________ ____________________

Why do animals make sounds? Write down two reasons.

1. ____

2. ____

4 Mystery tins

Shake three tins. What does the sound tell you about the object that could be inside?

Choose words from the box or use your own.

hard soft round flat big small

What do you think is in each tin? Write down your guesses.

Tin number	What does the sound tell you?	Guess what it is
1	It sounds like it is	I think it is
2	It sounds like it is	I think it is
3	It sounds like it is	I think it is

Extension

Pluck the strings on a guitar.
Circle two words that describe the sound when you pluck the **thinnest** string gently.

loud	**high**	**rough**
low	**soft**	**bang**

Circle two words that describe the sound when you pluck the **thickest** string gently.

loud	**high**	**rough**
low	**soft**	**bang**

Checklist

Read each sentence and circle a face for it. Like this:

I understand.

I understand a bit.

I need more help to understand this.

- I can say where sounds come from.
- I can tell different sounds apart.
- I can use words to say what different sounds are like.

5.2 Loud and soft

Practising my science language

1 Making loud and soft sounds

Finish these sentences about loud and soft sounds. Use the words "soft" or "loud".

When I clap gently I make a ________________ sound.

When I clap hard I make a ________________ sound.

When I whisper I make a ________________ sound.

When I shout I make a ________________ sound.

2 Listening carefully

Omar, Alec and Nadiya are listening to some sounds. Omar is closest and Nadiya is furthest away.

Who do you think says each of the following? Circle the name.

"I can hear a very quiet sound." **Omar** **Alec** **Nadiya**

"I cannot hear the sound." **Omar** **Alec** **Nadiya**

"I can hear the sounds easily." **Omar** **Alec** **Nadiya**

Practising my

science language

3 Listening in pairs

Listen to your partner whispering to you when you sit far apart. Complete this sentence.

When we sit far apart I cannot ______________________.

Sit very close together and listen to your partner whispering to you again. Complete this sentence.

When we sit close together I can ______________________.

Practising my

science language

4 Travelling sound

Unscramble the words so that these sentences make sense:

When the truck was close to the listener the siren sounded

u d l e o r ______________________.

When the truck was far from the listener the siren sounded

t o e r s f ______________________.

5 Word whispers

crash snap ring pop

Which of these words did you choose to start the game with?

____

Did you have the same word at the end? **Yes** **No**

Was it difficult for the last person to hear the word clearly? **Yes** **No**

What do you think was the reason? Circle your answer.

The whisper was too **soft** / **loud**.

Checklist

 I understand.

 I understand a bit.

 I need more help to understand this.

Read each sentence and circle a face for it. Like this:

- I know the difference between loud and soft sounds. 
- I can describe some soft sounds and some loud sounds. 
- I know how to make loud and soft sounds. 
- I can say what happens to a sound when I move towards or away from it. 

5.3 Protecting my hearing

Practising my science language

1 What can you hear?

Your teacher will play you some sounds.

- First, cover both ears.
- Now cover only one ear and listen again.
- Finally, listen with both ears.

What do you notice about the sound?

- Now use pieces of cloth to cover both of your ears. Listen to the sounds again.

What do you notice about the sound now?

Complete the sentences. Draw a line to the correct ending. One has been done for you.

When I cover both my ears	the sound cannot get to my ears easily.
When I cover one ear	I can hear better than when both ears are covered.
I can hear sounds best when	the sound is hard to hear.
Sounds are softer when I cover my ears with cloth because	both ears are uncovered.

2 Staying safe

How can this person be safer?

She can ______________________________

____

______________________________.

3 Make your own ear defenders

Think about which material is best. How much will you need?

- Draw a picture to show how you made your ear defenders.
- Label the different materials.

Now test your ear defenders.

What did you find out? Choose a word from each pair in these sentences.

- We played a **loud** / **soft** sound without wearing ear defenders.

We then put on the ear defenders and played the same sound again.

- It now sounded **louder** / **softer** than before.

Extension

Put these sounds in order from soft to loud:

- Write "1" next to the softest sound.
- Write "4" next to the loudest sound.
- Which sound is the louder of the two that are left? Write "3" next to it.
- Write "2" next to the last one.

☐ a secret whisper

☐ a performing rock band

☐ a car waiting at a traffic light

☐ a passing car

Look at the picture.

Name three sounds softer than the sound of a heavy truck.

1. ____________________

2. ____________________

3. ____________________

Checklist

- I understand.
- I understand a bit.
- I need more help to understand this.

Read each sentence and circle a face for it. Like this:

- I know that we hear sound when it enters our ears.
- I can say what can damage my hearing.
- I can say how to protect my hearing.
- I can say how hearing can help keep me safe.

Glossary

Write the meaning of these words in your own language.

damage

____

____

near

____

____

ear

____

____

protect

____

____

far

____

____

quiet

____

____

hear

____

____

safe

____

____

hearing

____

____

sirens

____

____

listen

____

____

soft

____

____

loud

____

____

sound

____

____

louder

____

____

voice

____

____

6.1 Parts of a plant

Naming the parts of a plant

Draw your plant.

Label these parts: **roots**, **stem**, **leaves**

Can you label any other parts of the plant?

Practising my science language

2 Different plants

How many different kinds of plant did you find? Circle the number.

1 2 3 4 5 6 7 8 9 10 more than 10

Practising my science language

Look at the pictures of the plants.

Look at the pictures that show a tree and grass.

Which two things are the same for the tree and the grass? Write them here:

They both have ______________________________

____

What differences can you see? Write one here:

____

____

____

____

____

3 Making a model plant

Work in your group. Make a model of a plant using pipe cleaners and thick paper.

- Draw around a leaf onto thick paper, or trace the outline here. Draw about five outlines.
- Cut out the leaf shapes.
- Use pipe cleaners to make a stem and branches.
- Attach the leaves to the branches.

How can you make the roots?

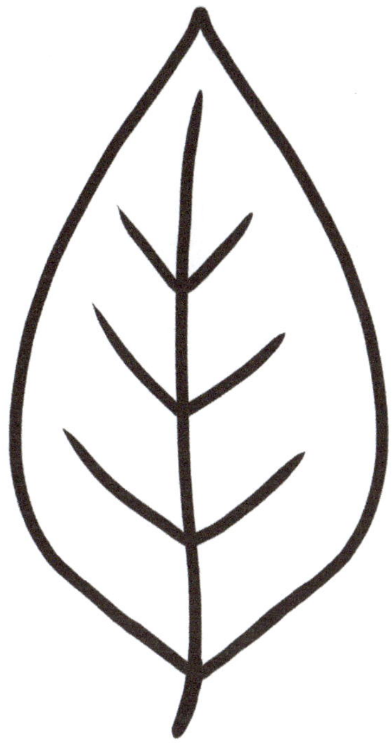

Extension

How can you tell that plants are alive? Choose a word to complete the sentence.

see hear grow move

Plants are alive because they can

_______________________________.

Checklist

Read each sentence and circle a face for it. Like this:

I understand.

I understand a bit.

I need more help to understand this.

- I can name the parts of a plant.
- I know about different types of plant.

6.2 Where do plants come from?

Practising my science language

1 Looking at seeds

Look at three seeds. Draw the seeds.

Write some words to describe each seed. Here are some words to help you.

An example has been done for you. This is the seed of a chestnut tree.

big small tiny
black brown
striped plain thin
fat round long

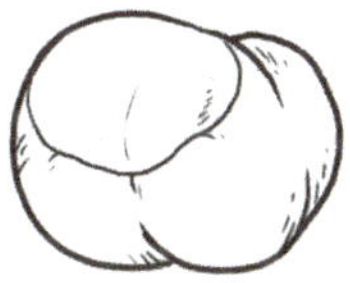

round, brown, smooth

Extension

Make sure the seeds are dry.
Use them to make a display.

Share your display with your class.

2 Ordering pictures

These pictures are not in the right order.

Write a number next to each picture to show the right order. Number 1 has been done for you.

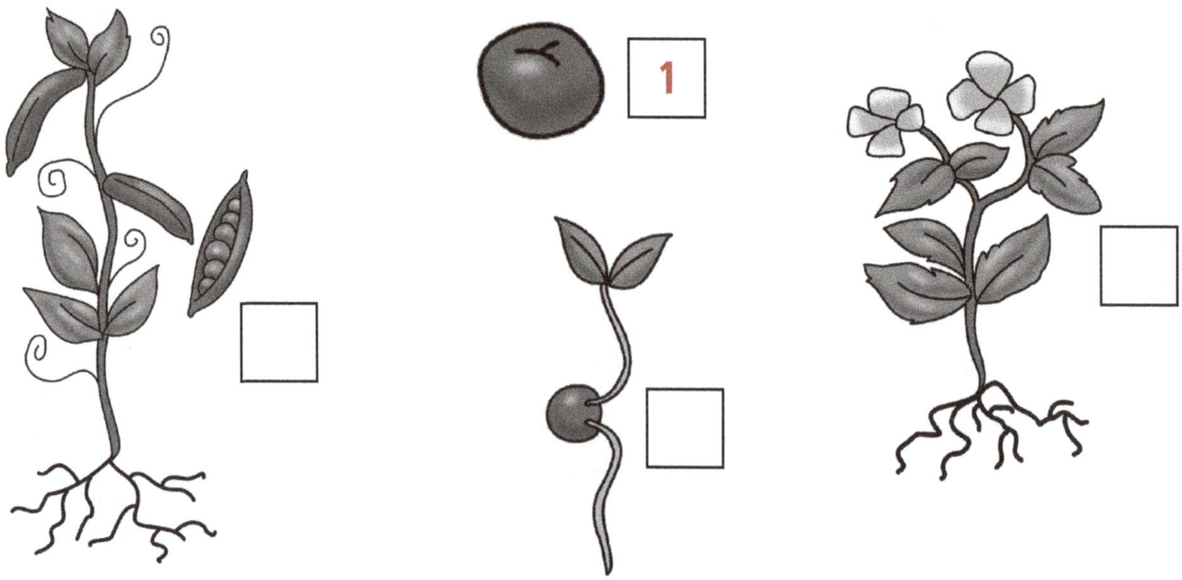

3 Watching how a seed grows

Check on the seed in the jar every day. Make sure it has water.

Draw what you see after a few days.

What parts of the plant can you see?

I can see the ______________________

____

____

____

4 Growing plants from seeds

Draw what you see after 10 days. Label the parts of the plant that you can see.

- Measure your plant with a ruler.

  It measures ______________________ .

- How tall is your plant after another week? Measure it with a ruler.

  It now measures ______________________ .

- How much has your plant grown from when you first measured it?

  My plant has grown by ______________________ .

5 Thinking about seeds

Write three things you have learnt about seeds:

1. ______________________________

____

2. ______________________________

____

3. ______________________________

____

Checklist

Read each sentence and circle a face for it. Like this:

☺ I understand.

😐 I understand a bit.

☹ I need more help to understand this.

- I know that seeds grow into new plants.
- I can predict why seeds grow.
- I know that seeds need water to start growing.

6.3 What plants need

1 Growing healthy plants

Water one plant every day for one week. Do not water the other one.

Draw or describe the two plants at the end of the week.

Plant with water	Plant without water

Extension

Start watering both plants. What changes do you see two days later?

____

____

____

2 Doing a fair test: Do plants need light?

Do a fair test to find out if a plant needs light to grow.

- You need two very young plants of the same type.
- Make sure both plants have water.
- Keep one in a dark place. Keep one in a light place.

Circle **Yes** or **No** in the table to show what each plant should have in this test.

	Light		Water	
Plant 1	**Yes**	**No**	**Yes**	**No**
Plant 2	**Yes**	**No**	**Yes**	**No**

Explain why this is a fair test.

It is fair because ______________________________

______________________________.

What did you find out from your test? Choose the right words from the pair.

I found out that a plant **needs /does not need** light to grow.

Practising my

science language

3 Remembering what you learnt

What did you learn about growing plants?

Complete the sentences using words from the word box.

water	seeds	grow	light	need

Plants

__________ __________

and __________ to grow.

Plants __________ from __________.

Draw around the sentences.

What shape do you see? ____________________________

✓ Checklist

I understand.

I understand a bit.

I need more help to understand this.

Read each sentence and circle a face for it. Like this:

- I know that plants need water to live and grow.
- I know that plants need light to live and grow.
- I can do a fair test.

Glossary

Write the meaning of these words in your own language.

fair test

plant

flower

roots

grow

seeds

leaf, leaves

stem

light

water